SOLOS FOR THE SANCTUARY
CHRISTMAS
2ND EDITION

12 PIANO SOLOS FOR THE CHURCH PIANIST

Arranged by Glenda Austin

ISBN 978-1-5400-5782-2

WILLIS MUSIC

EXCLUSIVELY DISTRIBUTED BY

HAL•LEONARD®

Visit Hal Leonard Online at
www.halleonard.com

Contact us:
Hal Leonard
7777 West Bluemound Road
Milwaukee, WI 53213
Email: info@halleonard.com

In Europe, contact:
Hal Leonard Europe Limited
42 Wigmore Street
Marylebone, London, W1U 2RN
Email: info@halleonardeurope.com

In Australia, contact:
Hal Leonard Australia Pty. Ltd.
4 Lentara Court
Cheltenham, Victoria, 3192 Australia
Email: info@halleonard.com.au

PREFACE

It is with great pleasure that we present you with another updated collection of *Christmas Solos for the Sanctuary.* Christmas and holidays mean different things to different people, but it is the only time that church pianists get to play the great songs of the season! From the classical leanings of "Angels We Have Heard on High" to the jazzy style of "Go, Tell It on the Mountain," I believe you'll find something suitable for your congregation or recital.

New selections in this edition include two lullabies: "Away in a Manger" and the seldom heard "A la Nanita Nana." The "Christmas Celebration Medley" is one that my sister (Gloria Sanborn) and I have played for YEARS as a piano/organ duet. It was a bit challenging to scale down as a piano solo, but it works! I've played every arrangement of this collection at my church, First United Methodist of Joplin, so they are time-tested and ready to go.

And as much as I enjoy each selection in this book, I probably have received more questions and comments about "What Child Is This?" than any of the other solos. It's quite different from what you might be used to hearing, and I consider it my *beatnik* arrangement (complete with light percussion playing along in my brain)!

As I write this in mid-July of 2019, temperatures across the United States are SOARING, some in triple digits. But *tempus fugit*—it won't be long before I'll be playing these again! I hope you'll be playing them, too.

Merry Christmas, and may God bless you as you use your talents to serve the Lord! "Each of you should use whatever gift you have received to serve others as faithful stewards of God's grace in its various forms." (1 Peter 4:10)

Glenda Austin

CONTENTS

A la Nanita Nana
(Hear Lullabies and Sleep Now)

Traditional Spanish Melody
Arranged by Glenda Austin

Not too fast, with a gentle rocking motion

con rubato

Pedal as needed

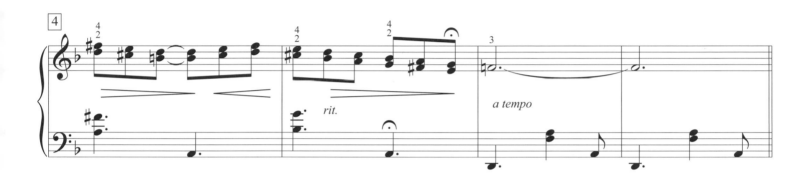

rit.

a tempo

mp

* Continue ⟨ ⟩ with rise and fall of melodic line.

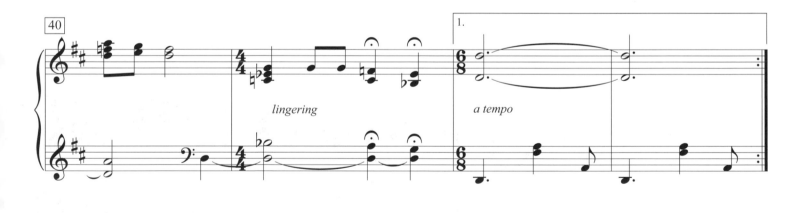

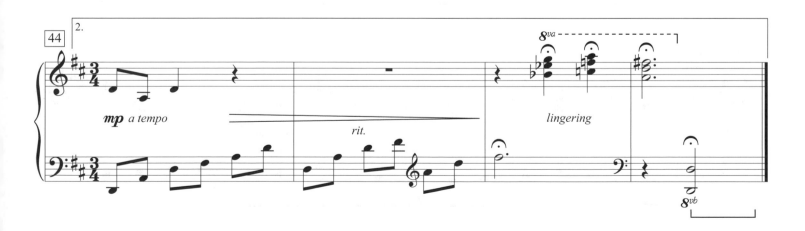

Angels We Have Heard on High

Traditional French Carol
Arranged by Glenda Austin

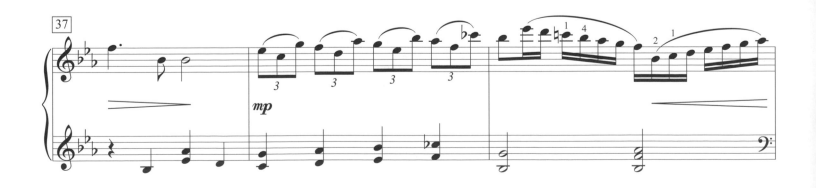

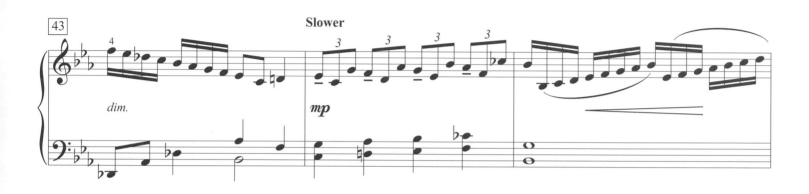

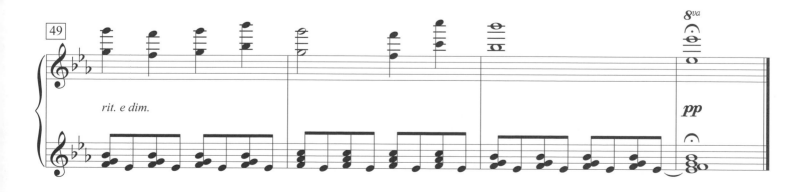

Away in a Manger

Words by John T. McFarland (v.3)
Music by James R. Murray
Arranged by Glenda Austin

Bring a Torch, Jeannette, Isabella

17th Century French Provençal Carol
Arranged by Glenda Austin

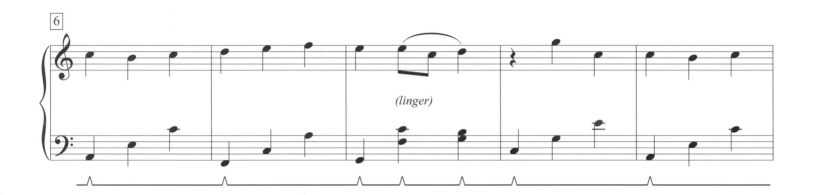

The First Noel

17th Century English Carol
Music from W. Sandys' *Christmas Carols*
Arranged by Glenda Austin

Christmas Celebration Medley
with Joy to the World / Silent Night / Hark! The Herald Angels Sing

Arranged by Glenda Austin
JOY TO THE WORLD
Words by Isaac Watts
Adapted by Lowell Mason

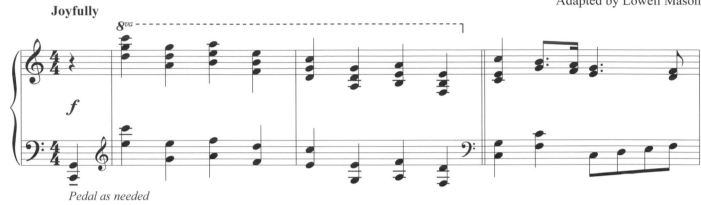

SILENT NIGHT
Words by Joseph Mohr
Translated by John F. Young
Music by Franz X. Gruber

A meditation

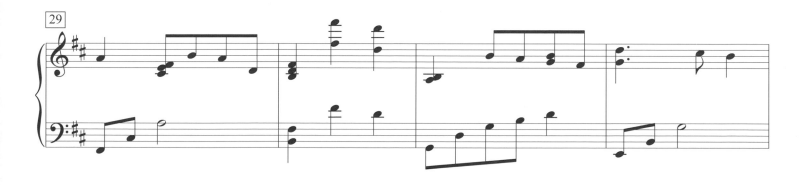

HARK! THE HERALD ANGELS SING
Words by Charles Wesley
Altered by George Whitefield
Music by Felix Mendelssohn-Bartholdy

Go, Tell It on the Mountain

African-American Spiritual
Arranged by Glenda Austin

God Rest Ye Merry, Gentlemen

Traditional English Carol
Arranged by Glenda Austin

In a classical style, crisp and even

(No pedal)

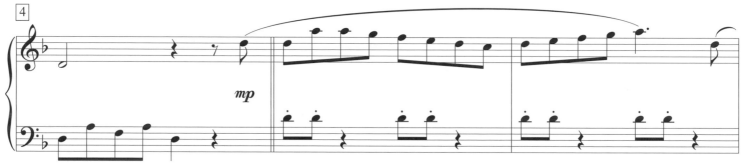

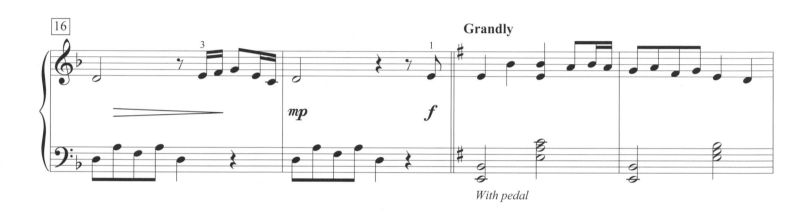

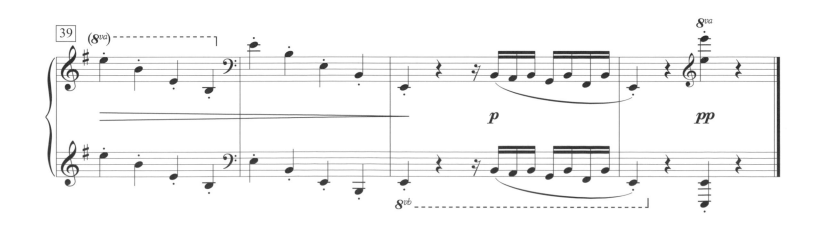

Sing We Now of Christmas

Traditional French Carol
Arranged by Glenda Austin

Briskly, in 2 ♩ = ca. 104

L.H. detached, unless otherwise indicated

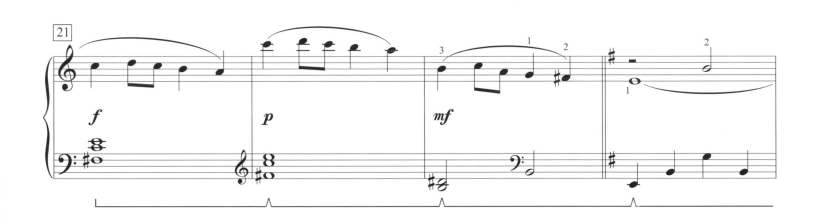

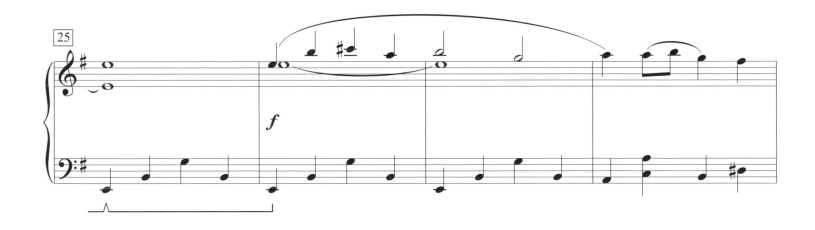

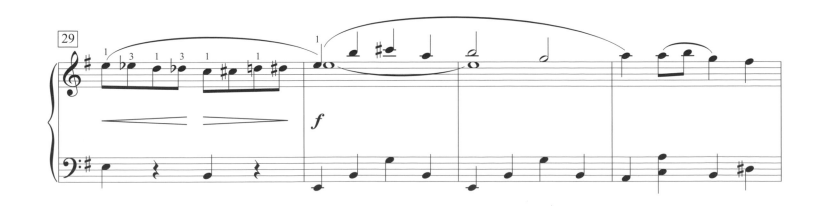

He Is Born

Traditional French Carol
Arranged by Glenda Austin

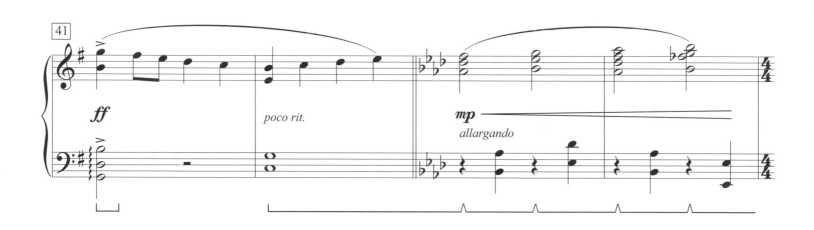

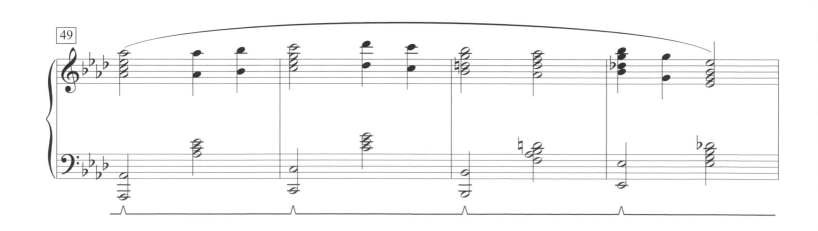

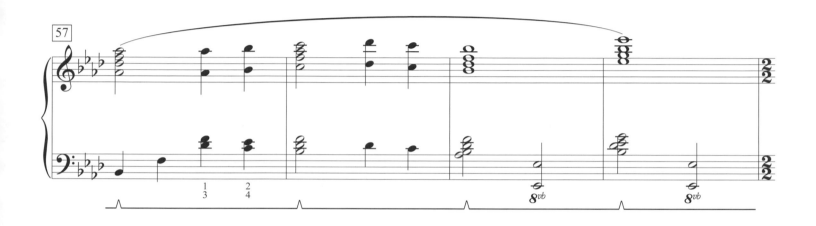

Tempo Primo ♩ = ca. 108

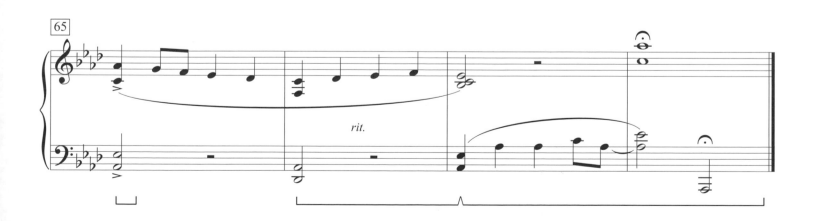

Infant Holy, Infant Lowly

Traditional Polish Carol
Paraphrased by Edith M.G. Reed
Arranged by Glenda Austin

Tenderly, molto espressivo

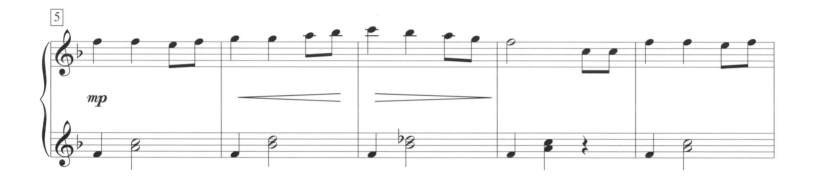

What Child Is This?

Words by William C. Dix
16th Century English Melody
Arranged by Glenda Austin

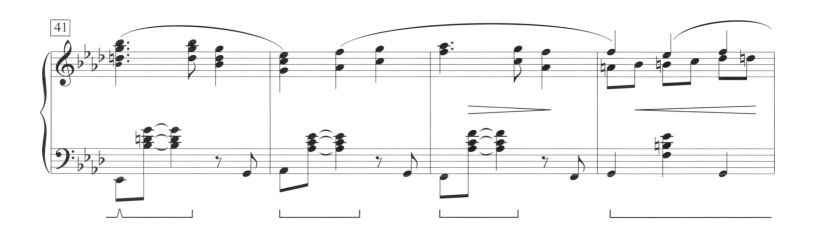

SOLOS FOR THE SANCTUARY

by Glenda Austin

Exciting piano solos for church pianists everywhere!
These excellent arrangements by Glenda Austin may be used for
church and recital performances, or simply for personal enjoyment.

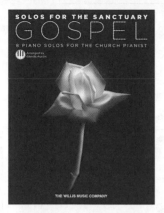

SOLOS FOR THE SANCTUARY – GOSPEL

8 Piano Solos
for the Church Pianist

How Excellent Is Thy Name/I've Just Seen Jesus/Because He Lives (Medley) • How Great Thou Art • The King Is Coming/We Shall Behold Him (Medley) • My Tribute • Mansion Over the Hilltop • Soon and Very Soon • Sweet, Sweet Spirit • Victory in Jesus.

00121443 ....$10.99

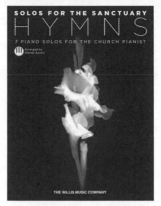

SOLOS FOR THE SANCTUARY – HYMNS

7 Piano Solos
for the Church Pianist

Amazing Grace • Be Thou My Vision • It Is Well With My Soul • Jesus Loves Me/He Keeps Me Singing (*medley*) • My Jesus, I Love Thee • Shall We Gather at the River?/On Jordan's Stormy Banks (*medley*) • What a Friend We Have in Jesus.

00416901 ....$9.99

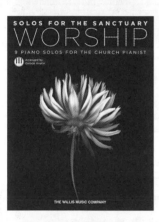

SOLOS FOR THE SANCTUARY – WORSHIP

9 Piano Solos
for the Church Pianist

Above All • Change My Heart Oh God • Give Thanks • Great Is the Lord • How Great Is Our God • How Majestic is Your Name • In Christ Alone • There Is a Redeemer • You Are My All in All.

00101918................................$10.99

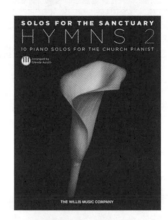

SOLOS FOR THE SANCTUARY – HYMNS 2

10 Piano Solos
for the Church Pianist

Blessed Assurance • Great Is Thy Faithfulness • Holy, Holy, Holy • Jesus Paid It All • Just As I Am • Nothing But the Blood • Praise the Lord! Ye Heavens Adore Him! • To God Be the Glory • Trust and Obey • Turn Your Eyes Upon Jesus/Softly and Tenderly (*medley*).

00295567..........................$10.99

SOLOS FOR THE SANCTUARY – SPIRITUALS

7 Piano Solos
for the Church Pianist

The Gospel Train • Joshua (Fit the Battle of Jericho) • My Lord, What a Morning • Rock-a-My Soul • Swing Low, Sweet Chariot • There Is a Balm in Gilead • Wayfaring Stranger.

00416897................................$8.99

SOLOS FOR THE SANCTUARY – CHRISTMAS

8 Piano Solos
for the Church Pianist

Angels We Have Heard on High • Bring a Torch, Jeannette, Isabella • The First Noel • Go, Tell It on the Mountain • God Rest Ye Merry, Gentlemen • He Is Born • Sing We Now of Christmas • What Child Is This?

00416488................................$8.99

Celebrate Christmas with Willis Music

Elementary

STEP BY STEP CHRISTMAS SONGBOOK – BOOK 1
Glenda Austin
Early Elementary
10 solos: Bells Are Ringing • Good King Wenceslas • I Saw Three Ships • Jingle Bells • Jolly Old St. Nicholas • O Come, Little Children • O Come, O Come, Emmanuel • One Shining Star • Snowing, Snowing! • While Shepherds Watched Their Flocks.
00278591 Book/Online Audio.....................$9.99

TEACHING LITTLE FINGERS TO PLAY CHRISTMAS CAROLS
arr. Carolyn Miller
Early Elementary
12 solos: Angels We Have Heard on High • Deck the Hall • The First Noel • Hark! The Herald Angels Sing • Jingle Bells • Jolly Old Saint Nicholas • Joy to the World! • O Come, All Ye Faithful • O Come Little Children • Silent Night • Up on the Housetop • We Three Kings of Orient Are.
00406391...$6.99

A YOUNG PIANIST'S FIRST CHRISTMAS
arr. William Gillock
Early Elementary
8 solos: Away in a Manger • Good King Wenceslas • Hark! The Herald Angels Sing • Jingle Bells • Jolly Old Saint Nicholas • Joy to the World • O Come, All Ye Faithful • Silent Night.
00416048...$3.95

CHRISTMAS CAROLS FOR KIDS
arr. Carolyn C. Setliff
Elementary to Mid-Elementary
10 solos: The First Noel • Hark! the Herald Angels Sing • I Saw Three Ships • Jingle Bells • Joseph Dearest, Joseph Mine • Joy to the World • O Come, All Ye Faithful (Adeste Fideles) • Pat-A-Pan (Willie, Take Your Little Drum) • Silent Night • Up on the Housetop.
00237250...$7.99

FIRST CHRISTMAS HITS
arr. Carolyn Miller
Mid to Later Elementary
8 solos: All I Want for Christmas Is My Two Front Teeth • The Chipmunk Song • Feliz Navidad • Grandma Got Run over by a Reindeer • A Holly Jolly Christmas • Mister Santa • Somewhere in My Memory • Where Are You Christmas?
00128892...$7.99

MERRY CHRISTMAS!
arr. Carolyn Miller
Mid to Later Elementary
8 solos: Away in a Manger • Deck the Hall • The First Noel • It Came upon the Midnight Clear • Jingle Bells • Jolly Old St. Nicholas • Joy to the World • Silent Night.
00416914 ....$7.99

CHRISTMAS TOGETHER
arr. William Gillock
Later Elementary to Early Intermediate Duets
20 duets: Angels We Have Heard on High • Away in a Manger • Jingle Bells • Lullay, Thou Little Tiny Child • O Christmas Tree • O Little Town of Bethlehem • Silent Night • Ukrainian Bell Carol • We Wish You a Merry Christmas • What Child Is This? • and more!
00237199...$9.99

CHRISTMAS CREATIONS
arr. Randall Hartsell
Later Elementary
11 carols: Away in a Manger • Carol of the Bells • Deck the Hall • God Rest Ye Merry, Gentlemen • Jingle Bells • Joy to the World • O Come, Little Children • Silent Night • We Three Kings of Orient Are • and more.
00416823...$6.99

THE JOHN THOMPSON BOOK OF CHRISTMAS CAROLS (2ND ED.)
arr. John Thompson
Later Elementary
Features lyrics, as well as the original illustrations by George Williams. 14 songs: Away in a Manger • Deck the Hall • The First Noel • Good King Wenceslas • Joy to the World • Silent Night • and more!
00414699...$7.99

For more Christmas and other seasonal music, please visit
www.willispianomusic.com

EXCLUSIVELY DISTRIBUTED BY

Intermediate – Advanced

CHRISTMAS PIANO SOLOS
FOURTH GRADE
arr. Eric Baumgartner
Early to Mid-Intermediate
10 holiday favorites: Blue Christmas • The Christmas Song (Chestnuts Roasting on an Open Fire) • Feliz Navidad • I Wonder As I Wander • Mistletoe and Holly • The Most Wonderful Time of the Year • Rockin' Around the Christmas Tree • Santa Claus Is Comin' to Town • Silver Bells • Some Children See Him.
00416790...$8.99

CHRISTMAS TIME
arr. Carolyn C. Setliff
Mid to Later Intermediate
7 classics: Carol of the Bells • Ding Dong! Merrily on High! • The First Noel • In the Bleak Midwinter • O Holy Night • Sing We Now of Christmas • The Snow Lay on the Ground.
00416713 ....$7.99

CHRISTMAS PIANO SOLOS
FIFTH GRADE
arr. Eric Baumgartner
Intermediate to Advanced
10 favorites: Brazilian Sleigh Bells • Christmas Time Is Here • The Christmas Waltz • Frosty the Snow Man • It Must Have Been the Mistletoe (Our First Christmas) • Let It Snow! Let It Snow! Let It Snow! • Rudolph the Red-Nosed Reindeer • We Need a Little Christmas • and more.
00416791...$9.95

SOLOS FOR THE SANCTUARY – CHRISTMAS
arr. Glenda Austin
Intermediate to Advanced
8 solos: Angels We Have Heard on High • Bring a Torch, Jeannette, Isabella • The First Noel • Go, Tell It on the Mountain • God Rest Ye Merry, Gentlemen • He Is Born • Sing We Now of Christmas • What Child Is This?
00416488...$8.99

JAZZ IT UP! – CHRISTMAS
arr. Eric Baumgartner
Mid-Intermediate
6 solos: Deck the Hall • God Rest Ye Merry, Gentlemen • O Christmas Tree • The Coventry Carol • Good King Wenceslas • Jingle Bells.
00416752 Book/Audio........$9.99

Prices, contents, and availability subject to change without notice.

WILLIS MUSIC

HAL•LEONARD®